DISCARD

COOL Sleeping

HEALTHY & FUN WAYS TO SLEEP TIGHT

Alex Kuskowski

A Division of ABDO
ABDO Publishing Company

visit us at www.abdopublishing.com

Published by ABDO Publishing Company, a division of ABDO, P.O. Box 398166, Minneapolis, Minnesota 55439. Copyright © 2013 by Abdo Consulting Group, Inc. International copyrights reserved in all countries. No part of this book may be reproduced in any form without written permission from the publisher. Checkerboard Library™ is a trademark and logo of ABDO Publishing Company.

Printed in the United States of America, North Mankato, Minnesota
062012
092012

Design and Production: Mighty Media, Inc.
Series Editor: Liz Salzmann
Photo Credits: Colleen Dolphin, Shutterstock

The following manufacturers/names appearing in this book are trademarks: Herb Pharm®, Kleenex®, Mead®, Pyrex®, Roundy's®, Sharpie®, Velcro®, Westcott®, Young Living®

Library of Congress Cataloging-in-Publication Data

Kuskowski, Alex.
　Cool sleeping : healthy & fun ways to sleep tight / Alex Kuskowski.
　　p. cm. -- (Cool health & fitness)
　Audience: 8-12
　Includes index.
　ISBN 978-1-61783-429-5
　1. Sleep--Juvenile literature. I. Title.
　RA786.K87 2013
　613.7'94--dc23
　　　　　　　　　　　　2012010347

CONTENTS

Catch some ZZZzzz's 4
Hit the Hay 6
Sawing Logs 7
Make Time for Sleep! 8
Stages of Sleep 10
Supplies 12
Good Night Cocoa 16
Fancy Face Wash 18
Slumber Spray 20
No-Fuss Neck Pillow 22
Drift Off to Sleep Playlist 24
Dream Log 26
REM Detective 28
Health Journal 30
Glossary 31
Web Sites 31
Index 32

CATCH SOME ZZZZZZ'S

Getting enough sleep is important. Sometimes you might feel too busy to go to bed on time. Don't be fooled! Getting enough sleep is one of the best things you can do for yourself. While you sleep your brain solves problems and your body gets ready for another day.

Sleeping well at night keeps you healthy and alert during the day. So make sure you get the amount of sleep you need. This book is full of tips to help you catch some z's. Check them out. Your mind and body will thank you!

Permission & Safety

- Always get **permission** before doing these activities.
- Always ask if you can use the tools and supplies you need.
- If you do something by yourself, make sure you do it safely.
- Ask for help when necessary.
- Be careful when using sharp objects.
- Make sure you're wearing the **appropriate** gear.

Be Prepared

- Read the entire activity before you begin.
- Make sure you have all the tools and materials listed.
- Do you have enough time to complete the activity?
- Keep your work area clean and organized.
- Follow the directions.
- Clean up any mess you make.

HIT THE HAY

It can take some practice to get your sleep **schedule** right. Most young people need eight to 10 hours of sleep. The best thing you can do is set up a **routine**. Do the same things each night before hitting the hay. Read a book, eat a snack, or wash your face. Pay attention to your body too. Notice what time you usually start feeling sleepy and make that your bedtime. If you get enough rest at night, you should be **alert** all day long.

REST UP!

> Go to bed at the same time each night.

> Write down what you're feeling so you can rest without worries.

> Exercise during the day to release energy.

SAWING LOGS

Snoring can happen to anyone, old or young! People snore when they can't breathe freely while they sleep. Snoring happens when muscles in the throat and tongue **vibrate** against each other.

STOP THE NOISE!

> Wear breathing strips on your nose while you sleep.

> Change positions.

> Don't eat a big meal right before bed.

LIGHT SLEEPER

At bedtime, turn off bright lights, such as the TV and computer screen. It will be easier for you to fall asleep. When you wake up, let the sun in! It tells your body that it's time to get going.

MAKE TIME FOR SLEEP!

AROUND THE HOUSE (INSIDE)

Sleeping is something you do at home! Make your room a good sleep zone. When you head to bed make sure your room is cool, dark, and quiet.

AROUND THE HOUSE (OUTSIDE)

If you have nice weather you can enjoy the fresh air. Ask an adult if you can camp out for a night in your backyard.

BED HEAD

Don't do homework, read, or talk on the phone on your bed. That way your brain will only think of sleeping when you are in bed!

PLUGGED IN

Computers are used for a lot of things. Most kids use them for talking to friends and doing homework. You can use your computer to research what your dreams mean.

ON THE ROAD

Car rides, especially road trips, can upset your **schedule**. Sleeping while traveling is a good way to catch up on lost rest. Before you know it, you'll arrive at your **destination**!

AT SCHOOL

Most of the time you can't sleep at school. It's where you want to be most awake! Talk with your teachers and friends about dreams. Or share tips for getting enough sleep.

WITH FRIENDS

Invite some friends to your house for a sleepover! Try some of the sleep-related activities in this book together.

STAGES OF SLEEP

STAGE 1

You doze in stage one. Your breathing slows and your muscles relax. Most of the time, if you get woken up in this stage you won't even know you were asleep!

STAGE 2

After a few minutes you slip into stage two. Your heart beats slower and your body temperature goes down. You also stop noticing your surroundings.

STAGE 3

Stage three is the start of deep sleep. Your brain waves change. It is harder for you to be woken up. This is the stage where some people might walk or talk in their sleep!

STAGE 4

Stage four is the deepest stage of sleep. It's really tough to wake up from this stage. If you do you'll probably be confused for a few minutes.

SWEET DREAMING

Dreaming helps keep you fresh and healthy. In dreams the brain works through daytime problems. Dreaming is also important for memory, learning, and creativity. Dream away! It's good for you.

SUPPLIES

Here are some of the things that you'll need to get started!

adult size long-sleeved shirt

airtight container

bar of unscented soap

cardboard tissue box (opening in the top)

CD (optional)

chamomile essential oil (optional)

cheese grater

cocoa powder

computer

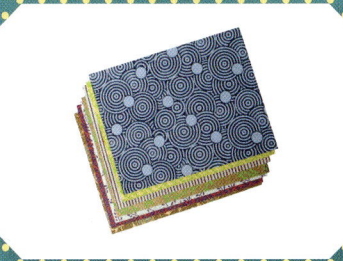
decorative paper

distilled water

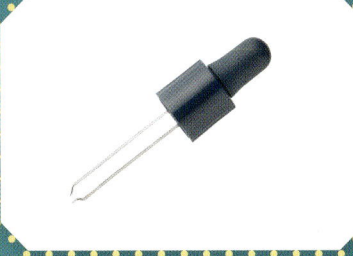
eyedropper

ground cinnamon (optional)

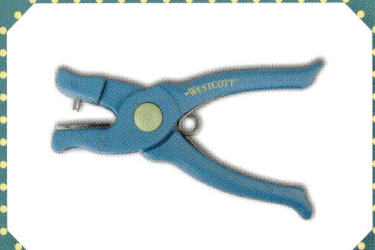
hole punch

hook-and-loop dots

isopropyl alcohol

13

lavender essential oil

measuring cups & spoons

milk

mixing bowls

mixing spoon

mug

music player

notebook

powdered creamer

powdered sugar

puffy paint

ribbon

ruler

scissors

small saucepan

liquid soap dispenser

spray bottle

stapler

Good Night Cocoa

 A soothing snack!

what you need

- 1 cup powdered creamer
- 2½ cups powdered sugar
- 1½ cups cocoa powder
- 2 teaspoons ground cinnamon (optional)
- ¾ cup milk
- measuring cups
- measuring spoons
- medium mixing bowl
- mixing spoon
- airtight container
- small saucepan
- mug

1. Put the creamer, sugar, cocoa powder, and cinnamon in a medium bowl. Stir until the ingredients are well mixed.

2. Store the cocoa mix in an airtight container. It makes about 15 servings of hot cocoa.

3. To make one serving of hot cocoa, put ⅓ cup of the cocoa mix in a small saucepan. Add ¾ cup milk.

4. Stir while heating the mixture on low heat for 5 to 10 minutes. Pour the cocoa into a mug. It will be hot. Drink carefully!

TIP: Try adding marshmallows, whipped cream, a stick of cinnamon, or a candy cane to your cocoa. Yum!

Fancy Face Wash

Feel fresh before bed!

WHAT YOU NEED

- 4-ounce bar unscented soap
- cheese grater
- large bowl
- ½ gallon distilled water
- large pot
- lavender essential oil (optional)
- eyedropper
- mixing spoon
- measuring cup
- liquid soap dispenser
- markers
- white sticker

18

1. Shred the whole bar of soap with the cheese grater. Put the shredded soap in a large bowl.

2. Put the distilled water in a large pot on the stove. Bring the water to a boil.

3. When the water boils turn off the heat. Pour the water into the bowl with the soap. If you want scented soap, add ten drops of essential oil.

4. Stir with a mixing spoon until the soap and the water are mixed together.

5. Use a measuring cup to transfer the mixture into the soap dispenser. Let it sit overnight.

6. Use markers and a sticker to make a fun label for your soap.

7. You can start using your soap the next day. Try washing your hands and face with it before bed.

Slumber Spray

 Let the sweet smell send you to sleep!

WHAT YOU NEED

- 1 teaspoon isopropyl alcohol
- ¼ cup distilled water
- measuring spoons
- measuring cups
- spray bottle
- lavender essential oil
- eyedropper
- chamomile essential oil (optional)
- puffy paint
- small funnel

1. Use a small funnel to put the alcohol and distilled water in the spray bottle.

2. Use the eyedropper to add eight drops of lavender essential oil. Add four drops of chamomile essential oil if you want extra scent.

3. Put the lid on the spray bottle. Make sure it is on tight. Shake it up. Use puffy paint to label and decorate the spray bottle.

4. When you're ready for bed give your pillow one spray. The scent will relax you!

TIP: Essential oils can be found at most natural health food stores. Essential oils should *not* be put directly on your skin! They can hurt you if not used correctly.

No-Fuss Neck Pillow

Get some shut-eye on your trip!

WHAT YOU NEED

- adult size long-sleeved shirt
- scissors
- ruler
- marker
- 1-inch hole punch
- 6 8-inch (20 cm) pieces of ribbon
- pillow stuffing

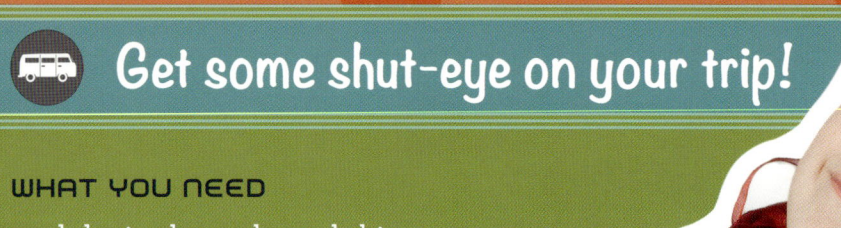

1. Cut off one of the shirt sleeves at the shoulder. If the sleeve has a cuff, cut it off too. Trim the edges to make both ends straight. Lay the sleeve out flat.

2. Measure two inches (5 cm) in from one end of the sleeve. Make a mark. Fold the end of the sleeve until the edge is even with the mark.

3. Punch three holes through the folded edge of the fabric. Make one hole near each corner and one in the middle. Make sure to punch through all four layers of fabric.

4. Tie a piece of ribbon through each hole.

5. Fill the sleeve with pillow stuffing. Repeat steps two through four to close the open end of the sleeve.

6. Put the pillow behind your neck when you are traveling. It will help you sleep better if you are sitting up.

23

Drift Off to Sleep Playlist

Set your dreams to music!

WHAT YOU NEED

- paper
- pen
- music or sound recordings
- computer
- music player
- CD (optional)

1 Make a list of calming sounds you like. Some people find classical music calming. Others think nature sounds are soothing. You could even include a favorite **lullaby**!

2 Look online or in your music collection for recordings of the sounds or songs on your list.

3 Make a playlist of the sounds or songs on your computer. Put the playlist on your music player or burn it onto a CD.

4 Listen to your sleep playlist as you fall asleep.

TIP: Keep the volume low. If it's too loud, it might keep you awake instead of helping you sleep!

Dream Log

Record your dreams!

WHAT YOU NEED

- cardboard tissue box (opening in the top)
- scissors
- glue
- decorative paper
- 10 sheets of plain paper
- stapler
- ribbon
- hook-and-loop dots
- markers
- white sticker

1   Open the seams of the tissue box to flatten it. Be careful not to rip it. Cut off the flap with the hole for the tissues. Cut along the fold.

2   Fold in the small side flaps. Glue them to the inside of the box. Let the glue dry. Glue decorative paper over both sides of the box. Trim the edges so the paper is even with the cardboard.

3   Fold the stack of paper in half the long way. Open it up again. Put several staples along the fold. Fold the paper again. Glue a ribbon over the fold. Let the glue dry.

4   Put the paper on the middle section of the box. See if the flaps can close around it. If the paper is too big, trim it until it fits. Glue the back sheet of paper to the middle section of the box.

5   Stick the two sides of each hook-and-loop dot together. Then stick them to the inside of the top flap. Fold the top flap over the bottom flap. Press firmly so the dots stick to the bottom flap.

6   Make a label for your Dream Log. Add ribbon for decoration.

27

REM Detective

Catch a dreamer red-handed!

WHAT YOU NEED

- friend, family member, or pet
- pen
- notebook

1 Ask a friend or family member if it's okay if you watch him or her sleep. You can also do this activity with a pet.

2 If your subject is a person, ask about his or her sleeping habits. How long does it take to fall asleep? Does he or she have a lot of dreams or wake up during the night? Write down the answers.

3 Then watch the subject sleep. Are his or her eyelids moving? If so, he or she is in REM sleep and is dreaming. Record how long after falling asleep it happened. Also record how long the movement lasts. It doesn't happen constantly. See how many times the subject goes into REM sleep.

4 If your subject is a person, share what you recorded with him or her. Wait until the subject wakes up, though! Ask if he or she remembers the dreams.

REM
REM stands for Rapid Eye Movement. That's when you dream. It can happen in sleep stages two, three, and four. Most people spend about 25% of the night in REM sleep!

Health Journal

Try keeping a health and fitness journal! Write down your sleep habits. Record how much sleep you get. Also include what you dream about, or what keeps you awake when you're trying to fall asleep. This makes it easy to look back and see how well you are sleeping. It could also show you where there's room for improvement. Decorate your journal to show your personal style!

Glossary

appropriate – suitable, fitting, or proper for a specific occasion.

destination – the place where you are going to.

lullaby – a song to quiet children or get them to sleep.

permission – when a person in charge says it's okay to do something.

routine – a regular order of actions or way of doing something.

schedule – a plan for when to do certain things.

snore – to breathe loudly when you are asleep.

vibrate – to make very small, quick movements back and forth.

web sites

To learn more about health and fitness for kids, visit ABDO Publishing Company online at www.abdopublishing.com. Web sites about ways for kids to stay fit and healthy are featured on our Book Links page. These links are routinely monitored and updated to provide the most current information available.

Index

C
Cocoa, activity for making, 16–17
Computer, dream research using, 9

D
Dreams/Dreaming
  activities about, 26–27, 28–29
  importance of, 11
  research about, 9

E
Essential oils, 21

F
Face wash, activity for making, 18–19
Friends, sleepovers with, 9

H
Home, sleeping at, 8

J
Journal, for health and fitness, 30

L
Light, and sleeping, 7
Log, of dreams, 26–27

M
Music, and sleeping, 24–25

N
Neck pillow, activity for making, 22–23

O
Outdoors, camping in, 8

P
Permission, for doing activities, 5
Playlist, activity for making, 24–25
Preparing, to do activities, 5

R
REM (Rapid Eye Movement), 28–29
Routine, for sleeping, 6, 8

S
Safety
  in doing activities, 5
  in using essential oils, 21
Scent, and sleeping, 20–21
Schedule, for sleeping, 6
School, talking about dreaming at, 9
Sleep
  amount needed, 6
  guidelines for, 6
  importance of, 4, 6
  routine for, 6, 8
  schedule for, 6
  stages of, 10–11, 29
Slumber spray, activity for making, 20–21
Snoring, 7
Stages of sleep, 10–11, 29
Supplies, for doing activities, 5, 12–15

T
Traveling, sleeping during, 9

W
Web sites
  about health and fitness, 31